GW01260263

ILLUSTRATED AUTOSKETCH

Ian Sinclair

David Fulton Publishers
London

David Fulton Publishers Ltd
2 Barbon Close
London WC1N 3JX

First published in Great Britain by
David Fulton Publishers 1991

Note: The right of Ian Sinclair to be identified as the author of this work has been asserted by him in accordance with the Copyright, Designs and Patents Act 1988

© Ian Sinclair 1991

All rights reserved. No part of this publication may be reproduced, stored in a retrieval system or transmitted, in any form, or by any means, electronic, mechanical, photocopying, recording or otherwise, without the prior permission of the publishers.

British Library Cataloguing in Publication Data

Sinclair, Ian
  Illustrated AutoSketch
  I. Title
  006.686

   ISBN 1-85346-181-4

Trademarks mentioned in this book belong, as indicated, to the following organisations.

AutoDesk Ltd,: AutoSketch, AutoCAD, DXF: Microsoft Corporation: MS-DOS; IBM Corporation: PC, CGA, EGA, VGA; Aldus Corporation; Aldus PageMaker; Intel Corporation: 8087, 80287, 80387; Hercules Corporation: Hercules graphics card; Hewlett-Packard Corporation: LaserJet; Zenographics: Metafile; ACS-APT Computer Systems Ltd.: PL-80 plotter.

Designed by Almac Ltd, London
Typeset by Chapterhouse, Formby, L37 3PX
Printed in Great Britain by
Martins of Berwick

Contents

Welcome

Using AutoSketch 3

You can produce drawings of professional quality on paper as large as your printer or plotter can handle. Drawings can include text such as labels, headings and the symbols of mathematics, music and other specialised applications. All this can be done using any PC-compatible computer.

To use AutoSketch

You need a video screen system capable of displaying graphics. AutoSketch can be used with any of the standard systems such as CGA, EGA, VGA or Hercules. You must have a mouse connected to the computer and the use of a printer or plotter.

For large drawings, it is an advantage to fit an expanded (not extended) memory board to your computer. AutoSketch 3 can use up to 2 Mb of such memory. For fast drawing actions, it is an advantage to fit a maths co-processor chip.

To save your work

You must use a hard disk. It is possible to work with twin 1.2 Mb drives, but for any serious purposes the use of a hard disk of at least 20 Mb (and preferably more) is virtually essential. Your drawings can be saved in ordinary format or in a special DXF format which can be interchanged with AUTOCAD. Text can be interchanged with a word-processor, and drawings can be exported to a Desktop Publishing (DTP) program.

How much detail

Drawings made using AutoSketch can show as much detail as your printer can deal with. Ordinary screen-painting programs can only show as much detail as can be seen on the screen, limited to about 72 dots per inch. Using AutoSketch with a laser or inkjet printer allows you to use up to 300 dots per inch, and with a plotter even finer detail can be achieved.

What sort of drawings

AutoSketch is particularly suited to scale drawings in which each centimetre on the drawing must correspond to some dimension (one foot, one meter, ten metres . .) of the real-life object that is being drawn. This makes AutoSketch ideal for room or garden plans, engineering drawings, plans for yachts, furniture, models, clothes or whatever you like. It can also be used for maps, and for items which need no scale like holiday charts, planning diagrams, electrical circuit diagrams and so on.

Starting

Before you can start using AutoSketch V.3 you need to install the program on your hard disk.

Installing the program

Autosketch 3 automatically creates a directory when you install it on a hard disk. Do **NOT** try to copy the AutoSketch files onto your hard disk, because they are held in coded form and are decoded during installation.

- Place the first disk into the A: drive and type **INSTALL** (press **ENTER**)
- You will be asked about disk directory names- accept the default of SKETCH3 by pressing the **ENTER** key.
- You will be asked to confirm whether or not your computer uses a maths co-processor chip (the INSTALL program senses such a chip, but you need to confirm).
- Remove each disk in turn and insert the next disk as requested.
- Confirm that you accept the changes to the AUTOEXEC.BAT file, and to the creation of a SKETCH3.BAT file at the end of the process.

Older versions

If you are using an older version of AutoSketch, you will need to create directories for yourself, and copy files. It is preferable to upgrade to AutoSketch 3, because it is noticeably superior to its predecessor, all of this book refers to the later version.

- If you did NOT opt, during installation, to have the AUTOEXEC.BAT file of the computer altered, you may find that the batch file that AutoSketch 3 creates does not work, so that typing **SKETCH3 (ENTER)** does not start the program. If this happens, either add **;C:\SKETCH** to the PATH line in the AUTOEXEC.BAT file or alter the SKETCH3.BAT file so that it appears as:

  set asketch=C:\SKETCH3\SUPPORT
  set asketchcfg=C:\SKETCH3
  C:\SKETCH
  SKETCH %1 %2 %3
  CD C:\

See any good book on MS-DOS if you need help with these alterations.

Configuring AutoSketch

AutoSketch must be configured (adjusted) for the type of mouse, type of screen and type of plotter or printer that you use. Configuration is done simply by selecting numbers each of several lists. Start by typing **SKETCH3** (if you have altered the SKETCH3.BAT file as indicated in Page 3) or by using **CD\SKETCH** (press **ENTER**) followed by **SKETCH** (press **ENTER**).

Pointer

Select a pointing device. For a mouse, select *Microsoft Mouse* because most other brands of mouse use the same system as the Microsoft mouse.

● Use any other number only if you are certain it applies to the system you are using. The use of keyboard keys (no mouse) is not really satisfactory.

Display

Select the type of *Graphics Card* your computer uses – check with the manual for your computer.

● Note that the menu displays the full names of these devices, but your manual is likely to use the initial letters only, for example, VGA for Video Graphics Array.

● Select colour scheme for a colour display. For monochrome (which is clearer to see) the only options are normal (black lines on white background) or inverse (white lines on black background).

● For colour displays, you will have several options of foreground and background colours. Reply Y to the *Activate scrollbars* question if you are using a mouse.

Printer or plotter

Select the printer or plotter you intend to use.

● If you are using a dot-matrix printer and your make of printer is not shown in the list, use the Epson option.

● Laser printers can usually be set either to emulate Hewlett-Packard Laserjet or PostScript standards. If you are using a plotter, it is most likely to emulate the Hewlett-Packard plotter.

● Select the most suitable option, and you will be asked to specify a model in more detail. Specify the connection method, usually parallel. If you use a serial connection, you will have to fill in details of the settings for the printer or plotter from its manual.

● Select the *name* of the printer/plotter connection. Use LPT1 for a parallel connection and COM1 for a serial connection.

Configuring AutoSketch

Select pointing device:
1. Autodesk Device Interface Pointer
2. Mouse Systems PC Mouse
3. Microsoft Mouse
4. Summagraphics SummaSketch
5. Keyboard cursor keys

Select display device:
1. Autodesk Device Interface Display
2. Hercules Monochrome
3 Hercules In Color
4. IBM Color Graphics Adapter
   (Monochrome mode)
5. IBM Enhanced Graphics Adapter
6. IBM Video Graphics Array

→

Select color scheme:
1. White background red text
2. Black background red text
3. Grey background dark blue text
4. Blue background white text
Activate scrollbars for panning? ⟨Y⟩

Select plotter or printer:
1. No printer/plotter
2. Autodesk Device Interface Plotter
3. Autodesk Device Interface Printer
4. Epson/IBM Graphics Printer
5. Hewlett-Packard LaserJet
6. Hewlett-Packard PaintJet
7. Hewlett-Packard Plotter
8. Houston Instrument Plotter
9. IBM Proprinter
10. Okidata Printer
11. Postscript Laser Printer
12. TI 800 Omni Printer

→

Select Printer model:
1. Laserjet
2. Laserjet Plus
3. Laserjet Series 2
4. Laserjet IIP
Select resolution in dots per inch
1.   75 dpi
2. 150 dpi
3. 300 dpi
Plot connection:
1. Serial port (XON/XOFF)
2. Parallel port or system printer
3. File
Connection selection: Enter parallel/printer/
hardware serial device name (e.g. PRN,
LPT1, COM1)

If at any time in the future you need to alter these settings, do so by starting AutoSketch as follows:
Type CD\SKETCH press ENTER
Type SKETCH/R press ENTER

Using the Mouse

Mouse selection

The mouse will have either two or three buttons on its top surface, depending on the make of mouse. Only one button need be used, normally the left-hand button.

- As the mouse is moved on the desk or mat the pointer on the screen will move so that it can be placed on words in the menu bar. The word will appear in inverse (colours reversed) to show that you are pointing to it.
- Tap the button (press and release it quickly). This is *clicking on the item*, and its effect is to activate the item that has been selected.
- The pointer in AutoSketch will be either an arrow or a finger, depending on the type of action last used.
- Clicking on the *Assist* work in the menu bar will cause the *Assist* menu to appear on the screen. This is a comparatively small menu of six items only. A letter/number combination, such as A6, means that pressing the **Alt** and **F6** keys together will have the same effect as selecting with the mouse. F6 by itself would mean the F6 key alone.
- Move the mouse so as to place the pointer on a blank piece of screen and then click. This will remove any menu from the screen.
- A tick mark is used when an action can be switched on or off. The tick shows that the action has been switched on, and if this item is selected again, the tick will be removed, showing that the action is off.

Dragging the mouse

Dragging is a mouse action that is done unusually in AutoSketch. The scroll bars are at the right-hand side and the bottom of the screen.

- Click on the box in a scroll bar. This will make that box follow the movement of the mouse (along the bar).
- The box is released when you click again (you do NOT need to keep the button depressed).
- This *dragging* action will move the drawing on the screen, either up/down or left/right. Some menus of Autosketch also allow you to see more items by dragging the box of a vertical scroll bar.

Using the Mouse

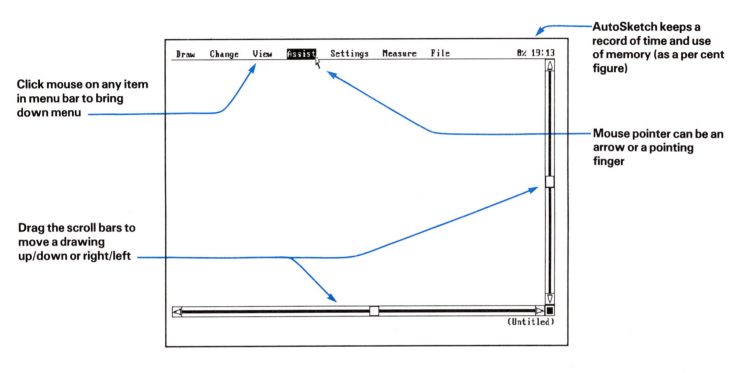

AutoSketch keeps a record of time and use of memory (as a per cent figure)

Click mouse on any item in menu bar to bring down menu

Mouse pointer can be an arrow or a pointing finger

Drag the scroll bars to move a drawing up/down or right/left

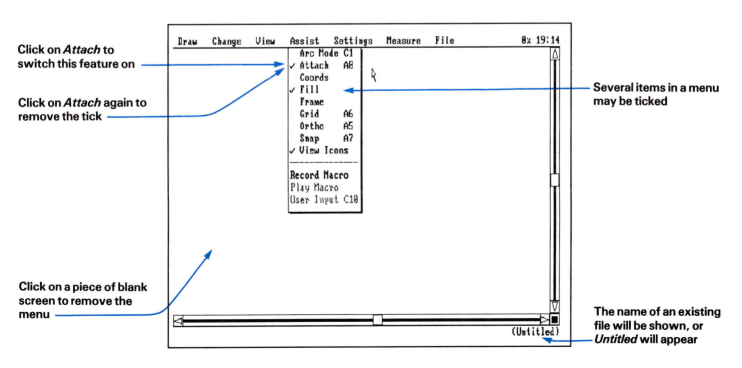

Click on *Attach* to switch this feature on

Click on *Attach* again to remove the tick

Several items in a menu may be ticked

Click on a piece of blank screen to remove the menu

The name of an existing file will be shown, or *Untitled* will appear

7

The Drawing Screen

Limits

AutoSketch deals with dimensions as numbers when you make a drawing, with no reference to units (feet, inches, metres, millimetres) until you come to print or plot the drawing.

- The drawing Limits box allows you to specify the largest range of dimensions on the normal drawing screen, but this does not restrict you to remaining within these limits.
- The usual convention is to set these limits to the size of the object being drawn, for example, if you are drawing a car with dimensions 5 m × 2 m, make these your settings.
- Concentrate on the numbers (your *drawing units*), not the measuring units. If you want to make diagrams on paper, set the Drawing limits to the paper size, but this is about the only example of using the paper size as the drawing limits.

Measuring Units

Use the Units menu to specify whether you want to work in feet/inches or in decimal units.

For any decimal units, which can be feet, inches, metres or any other units, select Decimal and specify the number of digits of decimals following the point. This is usually set by default to three.

- If you want to work in feet and inches, using fractions of an inch, select Architectural, and specify the precision from 1″ to 1/64″.
- You do not need to specify the units in detail with *Decimal Suffix* unless you want to print units as well as dimensions on diagrams.

The screen

The Drawing Screen contains the Menu Bar, scroll bars, and the arrow pointer. There are several options about the information that is seen on the screen.

- Lines will meet exactly only if *Attach* has been selected, or some other form of Snaps (see page 10) used.
- The grid of fine dots on the screen can be turned on or off using the *Assist* menu, and the spacing of items is determined from the *Settings* menu.
- The display of dimensions requires selection from the *Measure* menu.
- The display of co-ordinates at the foot of the screen is in terms of your *drawing units*, and is also switched on or off from the *Assist* menu. Coordinates are distances measured in drawing units from the bottom left hand corner of the screen. The X-coordinate is distance right(+) or left(−); the Y-coordinate is distance up(+) or down(−).

The Drawing Screen

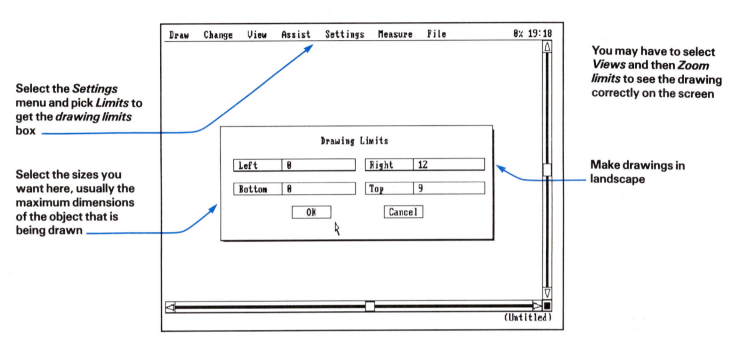

Select the *Settings* menu and pick *Limits* to get the *drawing limits* box

Select the sizes you want here, usually the maximum dimensions of the object that is being drawn

You may have to select *Views* and then *Zoom limits* to see the drawing correctly on the screen

Make drawings in landscape

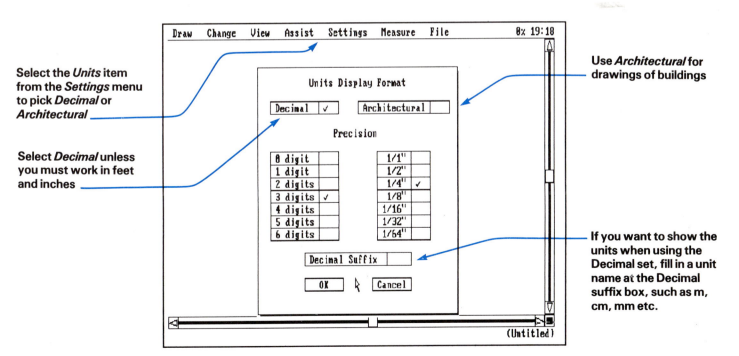

Select the *Units* item from the *Settings* menu to pick *Decimal* or *Architectural*

Select *Decimal* unless you must work in feet and inches

Use *Architectural* for drawings of buildings

If you want to show the units when using the Decimal set, fill in a unit name at the Decimal suffix box, such as m, cm, mm etc.

Grids and Guides

Before you can start creating drawings with AutoSketch, you need to know how to use some of the guides that make drawings simpler and avoid the need to move the mouse with great precision. The Ortho and Grid selections are two of these aids, and in the following pages we shall look also at Snaps and Attach.

Ortho

When Ortho is ticked from the Assist menu, it allows only horizontal and vertical lines to be drawn, no matter how the mouse is moved.

- These lines will print with none of the jagged edges that can be seen on diagonal lines, particularly when a dot-matrix printer is used.
- Use Ortho for applications in which the majority of lines are either horizontal or vertical such as: *Planning charts, Kitchen diagrams and other room plans, Bar graphs*
- Turn off Ortho by selecting it again.

Grid

The Grid is a more generally useful guide to positioning the mouse.

- Select *Grid* from the *Assist* menu.
- You will see a grid of faint dots on the screen.
- Alter the spacing between the dots by selecting *Grid* from the *Settings* menu to a value that suits the drawing size. Setting to unity will, for a 12×9 drawing, place twelve dots across the screen and nine down.
- Try a grid spacing of 0.25 as shown here or finer, but if the grid is made too fine it becomes difficult to work with.
- If the grid is too coarse, only a few dots may appear on a screen. A grid setting of zero (the default) makes the grid setting equal to the Snaps setting (see Page 12).
- Selecting a Grid does not force you to make each line in a drawing start or finish on that grid.
- The Grid is a guide, showing more clearly how far you have moved the cursor, and allowing you to move parts of a drawing into their correct positions, or draw them to correct dimensions.
- A Grid can be even more useful when you force drawn lines to start and finish on grid dots. This is done by way of the Snaps selection, (see Page 12).

For another guide select *Coords* from the *Assist* menu to show the cursor position in number terms. Once again, these numbers will depend on the limits that you have previously selected.

Grids and Guides

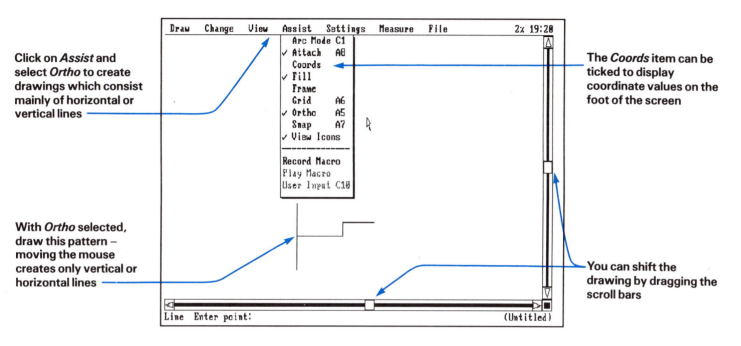

Click on *Assist* and select *Ortho* to create drawings which consist mainly of horizontal or vertical lines

With *Ortho* selected, draw this pattern – moving the mouse creates only vertical or horizontal lines

The *Coords* item can be ticked to display coordinate values on the foot of the screen

You can shift the drawing by dragging the scroll bars

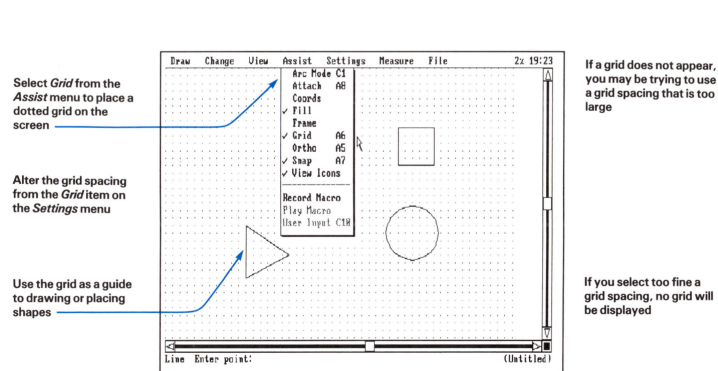

Select *Grid* from the *Assist* menu to place a dotted grid on the screen

Alter the grid spacing from the *Grid* item on the *Settings* menu

Use the grid as a guide to drawing or placing shapes

If a grid does not appear, you may be trying to use a grid spacing that is too large

If you select too fine a grid spacing, no grid will be displayed

Snaps and Attach

Attach

Select *Attach* from the *Assist* menu. This allows you to place either end of a line precisely.

- When Attach is switched on, you can draw a line to either end, or at the centre of an existing line, or the intersection of lines.
- A circle can have a line, or any other shape, attached at its centre or at any of four points around the rim.
- All shapes (see Pages 14, 15) have their own attach points to which another line end can be precisely located. Use *Frame* from the *Assist* menu to show Attach points for a curved shape.
- *Attach* is not always beneficial – you may want to draw lines to or from points other than the ends or middle of another line, for example. Use Attach only when you know where the Attach points are and need to use them. This is particularly helpful when you are constructing such drawings as electrical or electronic circuits and need to attach to the shapes that represent components.
- You can switch *Attach* on during the course of a drawing, even with a line half-drawn.

Snaps

Select *Snaps* to enforce precision of placing the cursor. When *Snaps* are selected on from the *Assist* menu, the arrow cursor is replaced by a cross marker. This marker can be moved only to snap points, which are by default the drawing unit points. For example, if your drawing is $20\,cm \times 15\,cm$, there will be 20 snap points along each of 15 lines, a total of $20 \times 15 = 300$ snap points.

- If you are working with Grid on, the default grid size will be the same as the snap size, so that your cursor will snap to each grid point. When you alter the grid size, however, this does not alter the Snap size. A separate menu action is needed to alter the Snap size, and for some purposes it can be very useful to have different sizes. It is often useful to have the Snaps setting closer than the Grid setting, half or quarter of the Grid setting.
- When Snaps are being used and the display of co-ordinates is on, the coordinates numbers will be simpler. For example, if you are working with $50\,cm \times 30\,cm$ limits and have Snaps set to 0.5 (meaning 0.5 cm in this case), then the co-ordinates numbers will take values such as 3.5, 10, 15.5 and so on, rather than the fractions with four places of decimals that you see when Snaps are not being used.
- Snaps are not always an advantage. If you want to start a line from the rim of a circle, for example, the use of Snaps will make this impossible except where the circle coincides with a snap point.
- For such an action, Attach in Tangent mode would need to be used rather than Snaps. Always try to work with Snaps on as far as possible, however, because this ensures precision which cannot easily be obtained otherwise. It is also an advantage to have *Coords* switched on along with Snaps.

Snaps and Attach

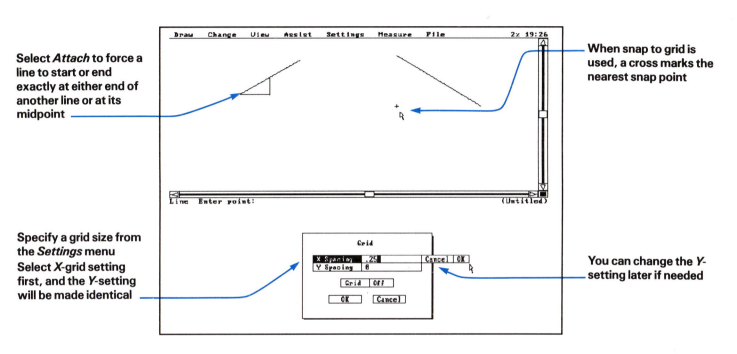

Select *Attach* to force a line to start or end exactly at either end of another line or at its midpoint

When snap to grid is used, a cross marks the nearest snap point

Specify a grid size from the *Settings* menu Select *X*-grid setting first, and the *Y*-setting will be made identical

You can change the *Y*-setting later if needed

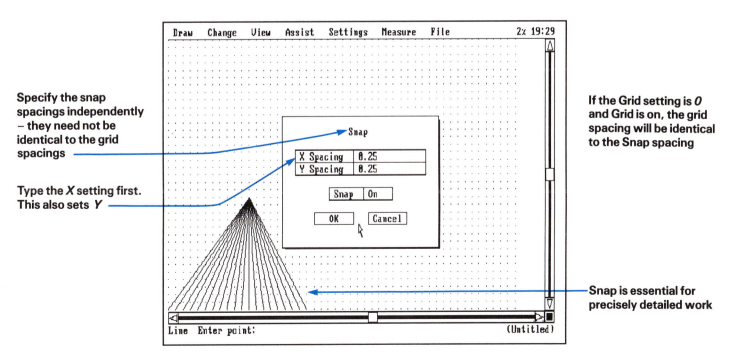

Specify the snap spacings independently – they need not be identical to the grid spacings

Type the *X* setting first. This also sets *Y*

If the Grid setting is *0* and Grid is on, the grid spacing will be identical to the Snap spacing

Snap is essential for precisely detailed work

Drawing Shapes

Start all drawing of shapes from the *Draw* menu – the same shape will be repeated until you make another menu choice. Always use Grid and Snaps on unless you particularly need to work without them. The *Point* option allows you to place a dot wherever you click the mouse button.

Line

- Select *Line*, position the cursor where you want the line to start.
- Click the mouse button and move the cursor to where you want the line to end. The line will stretch and change angle (*rubber-banding*) as you move the mouse
- Click to fix the end-point. Click again on the same point if you want this to be the start of another line.

Polyline

- This is drawn like a set of lines ending when the mouse is clicked on the starting point again.
- The difference between this and an ordinary set of lines is that a polyline counts as a single shape (see page 22), not as six separate shapes.

Box

- Click on one corner and then on the opposite corner to create the shape.
- The box will always have its sides vertical and horizontal, so that if you want diamond shapes you can either draw four straight lines, or rotate (see page 28) a box.

Circle

- Select *Circle* and click on the centre-point of the circle.
- Moving the mouse away from this centre point will draw a polygon (straight edges).
- When the edge is where you want it, click again, and the polygon will change to a circle.

Arc, Curve and Ellipse

- Select *Arc* and click on the starting point, then on some point on the arc, and finally on the end point.
- For *Curve*, click on a set of points on the curve, drawing a jagged line. This line will be smoothed into a curve when you click twice on the last point.
- For *Ellipse* click on the centre point and then on one end of each axis (the longest or *major* axis and the shorter or *minor* axis).

Drawing Shapes

Select *Line*, *Box* or *Polyline* from the *Draw* menu

Select *Line*, click on start. Move pointer, click on end

Draw the Box by clicking at opposite corners

Draw the Polyline by clicking at each corner

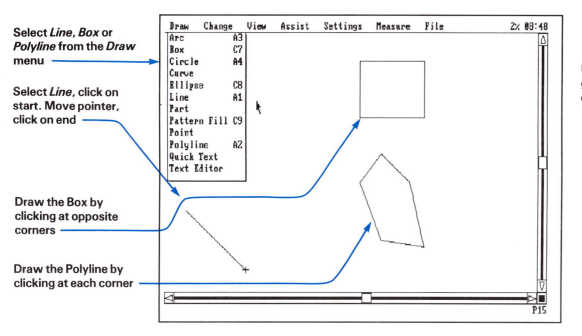

Use grid and snaps to guide you when you draw shapes

Select *Circle*, click for centre position. Move cursor to any edge point and click again

Select *Curve*, and click on each point (peak) of the curve, click twice on the last point

Select *Arc*, click on start-point, midway and on end-point

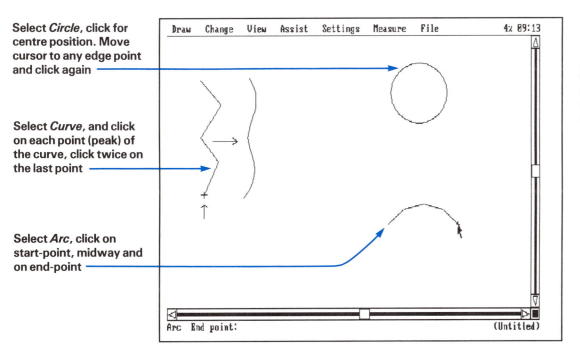

All curves start as a set of straight lines and appear as curves only when the last point is clicked twice

15

Holiday Planner

This is an example of the use of simple shapes, in this case, box shapes. In addition, it illustrates the use of text on a drawing, a point which will be dealt with in detail on page 36. Erasing parts of drawings is also dealt with later.

Planning the Planner

The planner will need twelve spaces for months and as many spaces for personnel as your needs dictate.

- Assign one vertical grid unit for each month and one horizontal grid unit for each name. This allows you to set drawing limits that will be 12 left-to-right (13 if you need to leave more space for names) and as many in the top-to-bottom direction as you have names, perhaps leaving some spares.
- Switch the grid on, allowing 0.8 unit spacing, and set *Snaps* to the same spacing.
- This allows a set of dotted lines (using *Line Type* from the *Settings* menu) to be drawn to indicate months. Reset the line type to solid after drawing these lines.
- Another option is to use *Ortho*, since all the lines are either horizontal or vertical.

Drawing the Planner

Start by re-setting Snaps to a closer spacing such as 0.1, allowing small boxes to be drawn – they need not represent weeks too exactly because the exact dates can be put in as text.

- Start drawing with a set of boxes, or with the names of the months.
- In this example, the boxes were drawn first, using *Coords* switched on so that boxes could be placed on lines that are equally spaced apart. This was followed by the text using the *Text* option of the *Draw* menu.
- This is a very simple scheme, and you might like to elaborate it with horizontal lines to divide the space between each person-line, with a large box to show when the greatest number of people will be on holiday, with a complete box frame, or in other ways. The main purpose of this example is to show how the simplest possible drawing action can be usefully employed.

Clearing the Boxes

The planner boxes can be erased selectively, leaving the text, (see page 22). This allows the framework to remain for another planner for the next year.

- You can also erase the text selectively.
- Some boxes can be left in place if a member of staff always takes the same weeks each year.

16

Holiday Planner

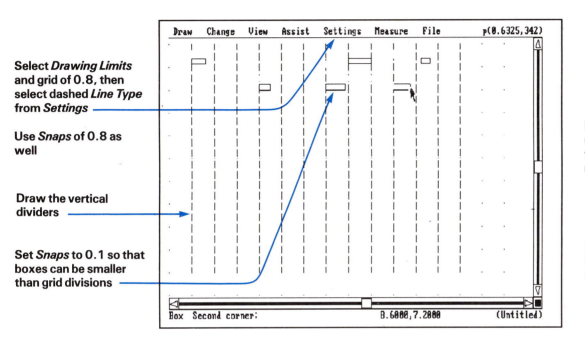

Select *Drawing Limits* and grid of 0.8, then select dashed *Line Type* from *Settings*

Use *Snaps* of 0.8 as well

Draw the vertical dividers

Set *Snaps* to 0.1 so that boxes can be smaller than grid divisions

Leave text until later unless you start to lose track of months and names

For the next year, these boxes can be erased and new ones put in

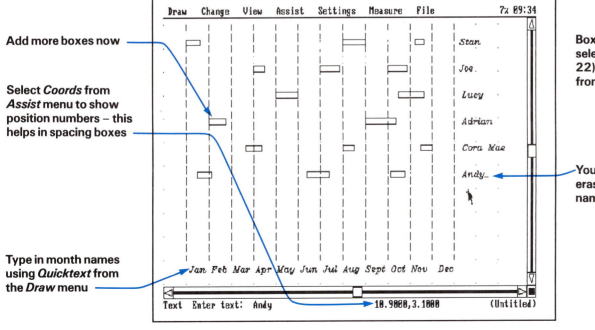

Add more boxes now

Select *Coords* from *Assist* menu to show position numbers – this helps in spacing boxes

Type in month names using *Quicktext* from the *Draw* menu

Boxes are erased by selecting them, (page 22) and choosing Erase from the Change menu

You might also need to erase, change or add names

Saving

When a file has been created using the *New* option from the Files menu, or when AutoSketch has been started afresh, the file will be un-named and all options will be at their default values. The *Save* option of the *File* menu is intended to deal with an already-named file, so that *Save As* is a better option. *Save As* also allows you to change the name of a file. This allows you to load a file, alter the drawing, and then save under another name. Get into the habit of saving a file with *Save As*, because this reduces the risk of erasing a valuable file when you have made some alterations to it.

Using Save As

When you take the *Save As* option, you are presented with the Save box over the drawing.

- Place the cursor in the name box, and type a suitable filename, (8 characters maximum, starting with a letter).
- Confirm that this is suitable by clicking on the **OK** box.
- Save the file by clicking on the other **OK** box at the bottom of the *Save As* box. You are given two chances to Cancel if you change your mind, and following the *Save as* action the drawing remains on screen undisturbed.

Using Save

Save should preferably be used when a filename already exists and you do not need to change it

- If you opt for *Save* using a new file, however, you will see the *Save as* file box appear, requesting a filename.
- Type a name of up to eight characters, and the file will be saved along with the other AutoSketch files. You can also include drive and/or directory in the name to save the file elsewhere.
- All drawing files are saved with the SKD extension letters – you do NOT type these.

Loading a File

- Select *Open* from the Files menu. You will see a box containing icons (miniature drawings) and names of existing files, in alphabetical order.
- Use the scroll bar in the Select Drawing box to display another set of icons and file names.
- Select the file you want by placing the cursor on the icon and clicking.
- Click on **OK** to confirm and so load the file.

Saving

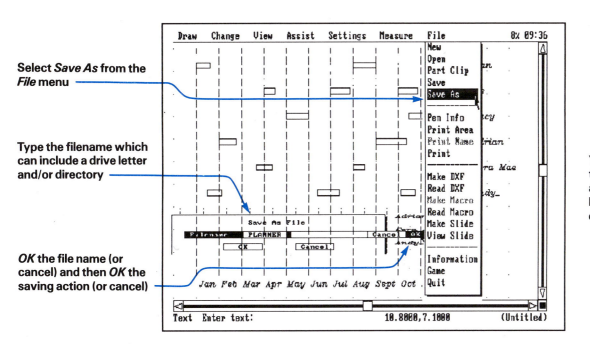

Select *Save As* from the *File* menu

Type the filename which can include a drive letter and/or directory

OK the file name (or cancel) and then OK the saving action (or cancel)

You do not normally see the *File* menu appearing along with the *Save File* box – this is a composite view

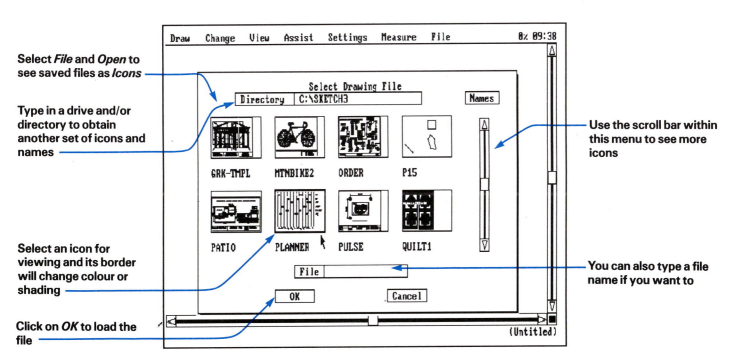

Select *File* and *Open* to see saved files as *Icons*

Type in a drive and/or directory to obtain another set of icons and names

Select an icon for viewing and its border will change colour or shading

Click on *OK* to load the file

Use the scroll bar within this menu to see more icons

You can also type a file name if you want to

Printing or Plotting

AutoSketch distinguishes between *printing* and *plotting* for the methods of printing out the drawing. For the best possible results a pen plotter, laser or ink-jet printer should be used. We shall concentrate on the *Print* options, because most users of AutoSketch are likely to use a printer.

The Printing commands

Selecting *Print* will print out the entire drawing on the selected paper size, you need only ensure that the printer is ready.

● To print only part of a drawing, or print on only a part of the paper you must create a *Plot Box*, which surrounds the drawing. Only the portion included inside the *Plot Box* can be printed, and though several Plot Boxes can be created, only one can be used for printing. The *Plot Box* is created from the *Print Area* menu.

Using Paper Size

Select *Paper Size* for one of two fixed paper sizes, the USA size of 8.5″ × 11″ or the A4 size of 297 mm × 210 mm; or to fill in your own values.

● You must remember that USA uses plotting units of inches, and A4 uses plotting units of millimetres. Unless your Drawing Limits have been set to the same as the paper size, you cannot use a 1:1 ratio of Drawing Units to Plotting Units.

● If you are using a paper size other than the two shown, fill in values for X and Y sizes (allowing a margin) into the spaces provided. You will be reminded not to fill in sizes greater than your plotter/printer can cope with.

● If the X size of the plot (as in this example) is greater than the Y-size, it is better to rotate the plot so that it is printed sideways on the paper. Click on the *Rotate by 90 degrees* box to change Off to On.

Scaling

Select scaling that will allow the whole drawing (or a suitable part) to be seen. You can move a *Plot Box* using the **Move** command, (see page 28) to cover a desired part of a larger drawing. In all cases, what is seen inside the *Plot Box* is what is plotted.

● You can also opt in the *Print Area* selection to create a *Clip Box*. This is another way of selecting a part of a drawing – only the portion that is inside both the *Plot Box* and the *Clip Box* will be plotted.

● The Move, Scale and Stretch commands of the *Change* menu can be used on both types of boxes. Click on **OK** to end selection.

● If you cannot see the *Plot Box* after completing the Plot Area page, select *Last Plot Box* from the *View* menu.

Printing or Plotting

The File menu contains *Print* or *Plot* depending on which device you will use – *Print* is shown here

Choose *Print* to print out all of the drawing

Select *Print Area* and fill in this form for special print sizes or part-printing

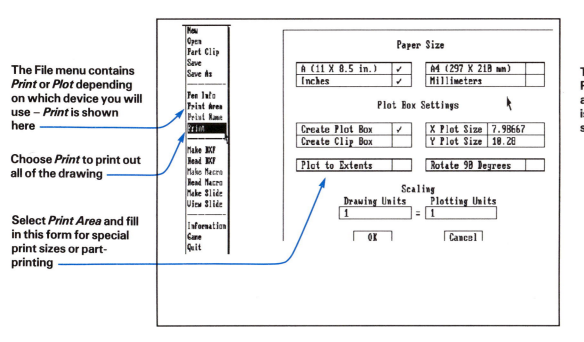

The form is used to set a Plot box or Clip box, or alter the scaling, which is: drawing size ÷ paper size

The Plot Box is titled and its size shown

The edges of the Plot Box show the edges of the paper

Select *Plot* or *Print* from the *File* menu to plot the drawing

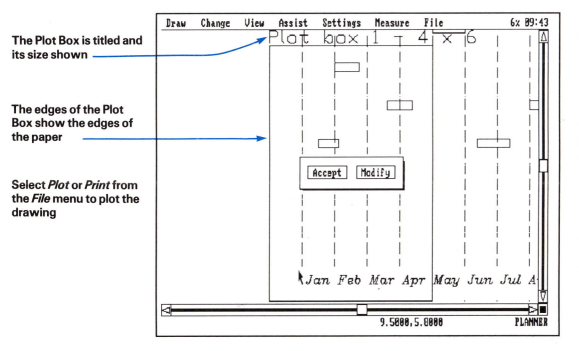

Each Plot box is labelled, and can be edited

You can have more than one Plot box, but only one visible at a time

Use the simple *Print* or *Plot* until you have more experience of AutoSketch

Change and Selection

Undo and Redo

Select *Undo* from the *Change* menu to erase the last-completed line or object shape. Select *Redo* from the *Change* menu, and the line or shape will reappear.

- You can keep selecting the options to delete or restore lines or shapes in order of creation or erasing respectively.

Selection

A single line or object is selected by moving the pointing finger cursor to any point on the object. Larger objects are selected by drawing a selection box, starting either to the left or to the right of the object.

- If the box starts to the left, only lines or other complete figures that lie entirely inside it will be selected.
- If the box starts at the right, any object which has any parts inside the box will be affected.

Property

Property means such items as line colour, dotted lines, layer, dimension units and text. All properties are initially ticked in the *Change Property* box; removing a tick prevents a property from being changed.

- The changes are pre-selected in the *Settings* menu, each bringing up a set of options, and the changes are made by taking the *Property* option from *Changes* and pointing to the object or selecting a set of objects.

Rotation

Select an object and click on a centre for rotation, then move the mouse so that the object rotates following the mouse. Another click fixes the rotated position.

Mirror

Select a shape to be mirrored, either touching the original or at some distance.

- Click the mouse on a point where the mirror image is to be placed and move the mouse until the mirror image is correctly placed. Click again to fix the position.

Scale

Change the size of a selected object fixing a point with a mouse-click and then moving the mouse to show the increased size. Another click fixes the new size.

Change and Selection

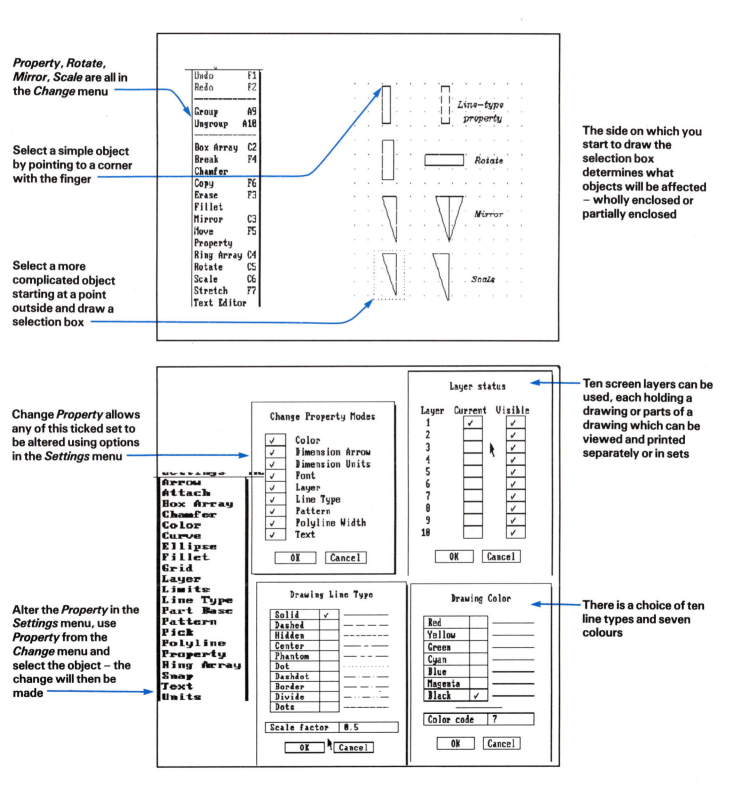

Property, Rotate, Mirror, Scale are all in the Change menu

Select a simple object by pointing to a corner with the finger

Select a more complicated object starting at a point outside and draw a selection box

Undo	F1
Redo	F2
Group	A9
Ungroup	A10
Box Array	C2
Break	F4
Chamfer	
Copy	F6
Erase	F3
Fillet	
Mirror	C3
Move	F5
Property	
Ring Array	C4
Rotate	C5
Scale	C6
Stretch	F7
Text Editor	

Line-type property

Rotate

Mirror

Scale

The side on which you start to draw the selection box determines what objects will be affected – wholly enclosed or partially enclosed

Change *Property* allows any of this ticked set to be altered using options in the *Settings* menu

Change Property Modes

✓	Color
✓	Dimension Arrow
✓	Dimension Units
✓	Font
✓	Layer
✓	Line Type
✓	Pattern
✓	Polyline Width
✓	Text

OK   Cancel

Layer status

Layer	Current	Visible
1	✓	✓
2		✓
3		✓
4		✓
5		✓
6		✓
7		✓
8		✓
9		✓
10		✓

OK   Cancel

Ten screen layers can be used, each holding a drawing or parts of a drawing which can be viewed and printed separately or in sets

Settings
Arrow
Attach
Box Array
Chamfer
Color
Curve
Ellipse
Fillet
Grid
Layer
Limits
Line Type
Part Base
Pattern
Pick
Polyline
Property
Ring Array
Snap
Text
Units

Alter the *Property* in the *Settings* menu, use *Property* from the *Change* menu and select the object – the change will then be made

Drawing Line Type

Solid	✓	———
Dashed		―――――
Hidden		---------
Center		—— – ——
Phantom		—— — ——
Dot		·········
Dashdot		—·—·—·—
Border		—— – ——
Divide		—— ·· ——
Dots		

Scale factor   0.5

OK   Cancel

Drawing Color

Red		———
Yellow		———
Green		———
Cyan		———
Blue		———
Magenta		———
Black	✓	———

Color code   7

OK   Cancel

There is a choice of ten line types and seven colours

Groups and Parts

Groups

A drawing of an object, whether it is a full drawing or a detail of a full drawing, will normally consist of a set of lines and other shapes. These are considered as separate items and can be erased, copied, moved, etc. separately.

- Such items can be grouped, making each into a single entity which AutoSketch treats as it would treat one line, selected as a single item. Individual portions of a grouped object cannot be singled out for erasure or other changes unless the whole object is ungrouped. Both *Group* and *Ungroup* are options in the *Changes* menu.
- Even fairly trivial objects in a drawing should be grouped because this ensures that they will always be treated as complete objects and there is no risk of accidentally selecting a single part of the object by mistake.

Parts

An object, usually one that has been grouped, may be needed in many drawings. You might, for example, want to make electronic circuit diagrams, using a standard set of symbols; another use is for architectural symbols. Most drawing applications, in fact, require a set of components or parts which are standard – though it might be necessary to alter their sizes in different drawings.

- Any object which has been drawn, or even a complete drawing, can be saved as a Part.
- Some point of the object should be designated as the *Part Base*, using the *Settings* menu. This forms a point for manipulating the object. The Part Base for a complete drawing is the bottom left hand corner unless you select otherwise.
- The object can be drawn alone, with nothing else on the screen, and saved in the usual way, or it can be a portion of a larger drawing and saved using *Part Clip*.
- When the Part is needed, the *Part* option from the *Draw* menu is selected. This gives a list of all files, with icons, and the icon for the Part can be selected. A pointing finger will appear, and the Part Base will be located at the end of the finger, so that this can be moved to any part of a new drawing.
- It is possible to buy disks of ready-made part files for popular symbols such as Electrical or Architectural. If you make your own Parts you will need to ensure that they are created in a size that will be useful, and all to the same scale.
- For example, a simple way of creating a collection of Electronics Parts is to draw a circuit with as many types of components as possible, and save each component as a Clip Part. If you use names such as ER, EC, EL, ET1, ET2 and so on, prefixing each Part name with the same letter, all of these parts will be arranged together in the Icon list.

Groups and Parts

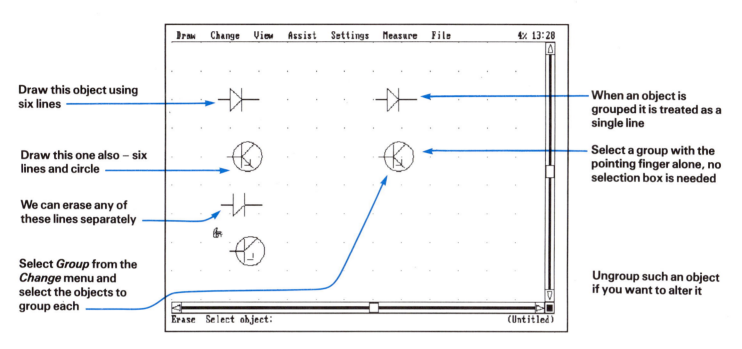

Draw this object using six lines

Draw this one also – six lines and circle

We can erase any of these lines separately

Select *Group* from the *Change* menu and select the objects to group each

When an object is grouped it is treated as a single line

Select a group with the pointing finger alone, no selection box is needed

Ungroup such an object if you want to alter it

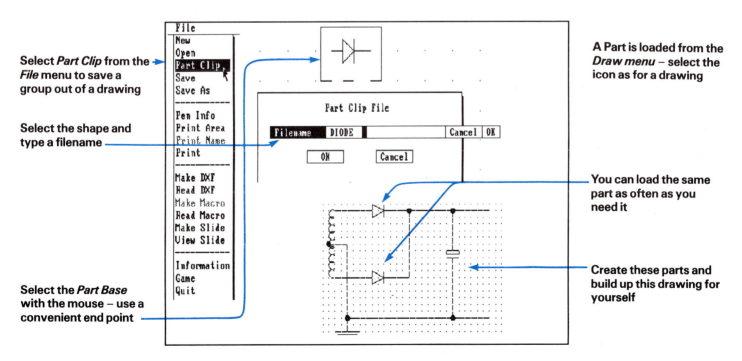

Select *Part Clip* from the *File* menu to save a group out of a drawing

Select the shape and type a filename

Select the *Part Base* with the mouse – use a convenient end point

A Part is loaded from the *Draw menu* – select the icon as for a drawing

You can load the same part as often as you need it

Create these parts and build up this drawing for yourself

Arrays

An array is a set of identical objects, and AutoSketch allows two types to be created, box arrays in which the objects are arranged in rows and columns, and Ring arrays in which objects are arranged around a circle.

Box Array

- Select *Box Array* to make a small array (one more row and one more column). Click on the object to be used, and point to some part of the object.
- Point to where the next copy of this point should be to the left or right (column point) and then repeat with the vertical positions (row point).
- At the last click, the array will be formed.
- For larger arrays, select *Box Array* from the *Settings* menu. This allows you to specify the array in any one of a number of ways. You can either specify row and column separation in numbers, or by pointing with the mouse (tick the *Point* box).
- You can also opt to fit a specified number of rows and columns with the objects, an easy way of creating large arrays. Altering the baseline angle will tilt the objects with respect to the horizontal.
- Remember that dimensions for arrays are in terms of the drawing unit. For example, if the spacing of grid lines is 0.2 drawing units, then an array dimension of one grid spacing is typed as 0.2

Ring Array

- Select Ring Array to draw a set of objects arranged in a circle.
- This requires you to specify **either** the number of objects in the ring or the angle between them (not both). You can type the co-ordinates of the centre, or select *Point* so that the centre can be selected with the mouse.
- The objects can be rotated so that one axis will always lie along a radius of the circle, or they can be left as they are so that the objects are always facing the same way with respect to the grid lines. You can select a pivot point, which is the part of the object which will always be placed on the rim of the circle of rotation.
- As each array is created, you are asked to opt for Accept or Modify, and even if you Accept and later regret it, you can use the *Undo* facility to remove the array.
- Try as examples bricks in a wall and spokes of a wheel.

Arrays

Select *Box array* to draw multiple blocks of objects

Use the mouse to pull to one side for a new column and down for a new row- you can choose to Accept or Modify

Select *Box array* settings for larger arrays

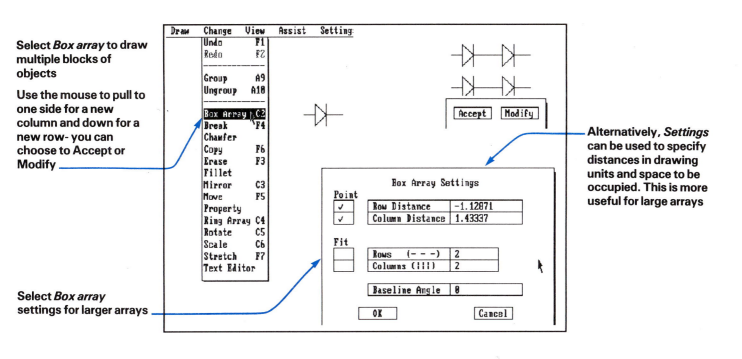

Alternatively, *Settings* can be used to specify distances in drawing units and space to be occupied. This is more useful for large arrays

Select *Ring Array* after typing in the settings that are needed

Check *Point* to allow centre to be selected by mouse

Check *Rotate as Copied* to change angle of each object in array

Now draw your Ring Array

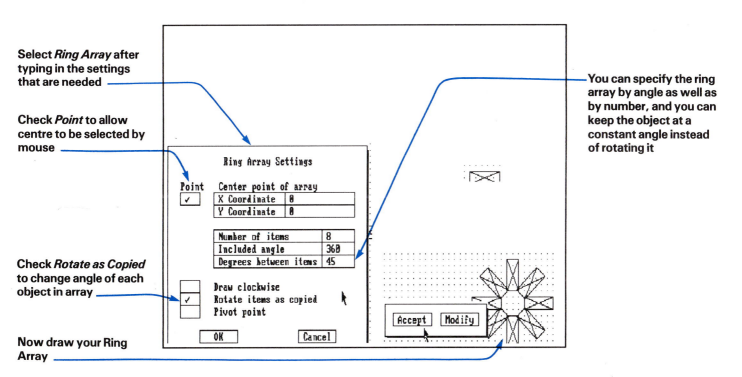

You can specify the ring array by angle as well as by number, and you can keep the object at a constant angle instead of rotating it

Move, Copy, Stretch

Move and Copy

Move and Copy both make a new copy of an object at another position, but when Move has been selected, the original is deleted.

- Select the command, point to the object (single item or group) or throw a box round it (a set of lines, not grouped), then click on a point on the object.
- Move the cursor to wherever the new position for that point is to be placed, and click to complete the action.

Stretch

The stretch command allows any object to have its dimensions stretched in any direction. Whether the object is grouped or not, stretch first requires a selection box to be placed, not surrounding the whole object.

- If the selection box encloses the whole object, a Move will be carried out instead of a stretch.
- Enclose only the parts which are to be moved, leaving the remainder in place, and stretching the lines to fill the space in-between. When the selection box has been drawn, select a point to move and stretch by moving the mouse to a new position.
- The image will show the stretch effect, which need not be in a horizontal or vertical plane, it can be in any direction. When the mouse button is clicked again, the final image will appear stretched to the new size.
- If you want to stretch an object in both dimensions, Scale is more suitable.

Break

Break is used to remove parts of a line, circle, curve or arc – it cannot be used on a Group, so that a grouped object should be ungrouped before attempting to use Break.

- Break is particularly useful when it is easier to make a drawing by removing parts than by building them up. For example, it is easier to draw a room as a box and then use Break to show the door aperture, than to draw the lines for the three sides and up to each side of the door.
- Start by clicking on a point in the line to be broken – do not choose a point where lines meet in case the wrong line is broken.
- Click at one end of the break, followed by clicking at the other end. This breaks the line, leaving a gap.
- When a circle or other closed object is broken, the break action extends anticlockwise from the first break point to the second.

Move, Copy, Stretch

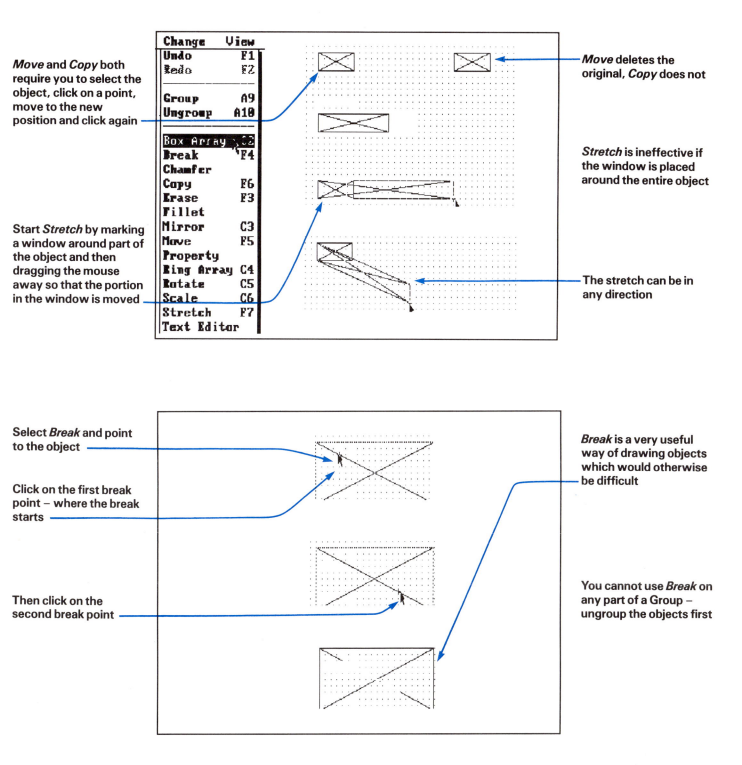

Move and *Copy* both require you to select the object, click on a point, move to the new position and click again

Start *Stretch* by marking a window around part of the object and then dragging the mouse away so that the portion in the window is moved

Change	View	
Undo	F1	
Redo	F2	
Group	A9	
Ungroup	A10	
Box Array	C2	
Break	F4	
Chamfer		
Copy	F6	
Erase	F3	
Fillet		
Mirror	C3	
Move	F5	
Property		
Ring Array	C4	
Rotate	C5	
Scale	C6	
Stretch	F7	
Text Editor		

Move deletes the original, *Copy* does not

Stretch is ineffective if the window is placed around the entire object

The stretch can be in any direction

Select *Break* and point to the object

Click on the first break point – where the break starts

Then click on the second break point

Break is a very useful way of drawing objects which would otherwise be difficult

You cannot use *Break* on any part of a Group – ungroup the objects first

Kitchen Outline

Draw this plan on four layers. Use *Layer 1* for the outline, the others for the details and lettering. This allows the layers to be viewed separately and even printed separately, and also makes it easy to alter the position of furnishings with no risk of altering the room drawing itself. Draw the bare room first and save this file to be used as a part for the complete diagram. This also allows the same room shape to be used as many times as will be needed (on an estate, for example) The same principles apply to garden plans.

The main layer – preparation

The main layer, *Layer 1* is by default the current layer.

- Check the *Layer Status* box from the *Settings* menu, which will also show that all of the layers are visible but only one layer can be current at a given time.
- Draw the kitchen outline on this layer. Make the drawing limits slightly larger than the kitchen size to allow for text placed outside the walls – this space can be used to show precise dimensions, for example.
- Use units of millimetres, as required by modern building specifications, and set drawing limits of 3900×3050 mm. Select the *View* menu followed by *Zoom Limits* to make this display correctly.
- Set *Grid* and *Snaps* to 50, meaning in this case, 50 mm (5 cm). This implies that items of kitchen hardware will be shown to the nearest 5 cm, but by using *Zooms* (see page 34) with a closer *Snaps* setting, more exact measurements can be used.
- The furnishings can be created separately on a magnified view and imported as Parts. Switch on *Coords* from the *Assist* menu in order to make it easy to follow the sizes.

Drawing the kitchen outline

Draw the kitchen as a box, with the door openings made by using *Break*.

- When this is done, **remember** to point to a part of the line that is to be removed when asked to point to the object. If you point to another part of the box, you can find that the whole box is deleted apart from the door, not what you intended (use Undo to restore the walls).
- **Remember** also that the *Break* action on a box moves anticlockwise.
- Draw the arc of the doors using a dotted line, selecting *Line Type* from *Settings*. Alter the scale factor to 100 to suit the drawing limits (default is 0.5) – you know when your scale is suitable by looking at the examples of lines in the menu.
- Draw circles centred at one door-post, then break, moving anticlockwise from the first break point to the second. Doors can also be dotted in.

Kitchen Outline

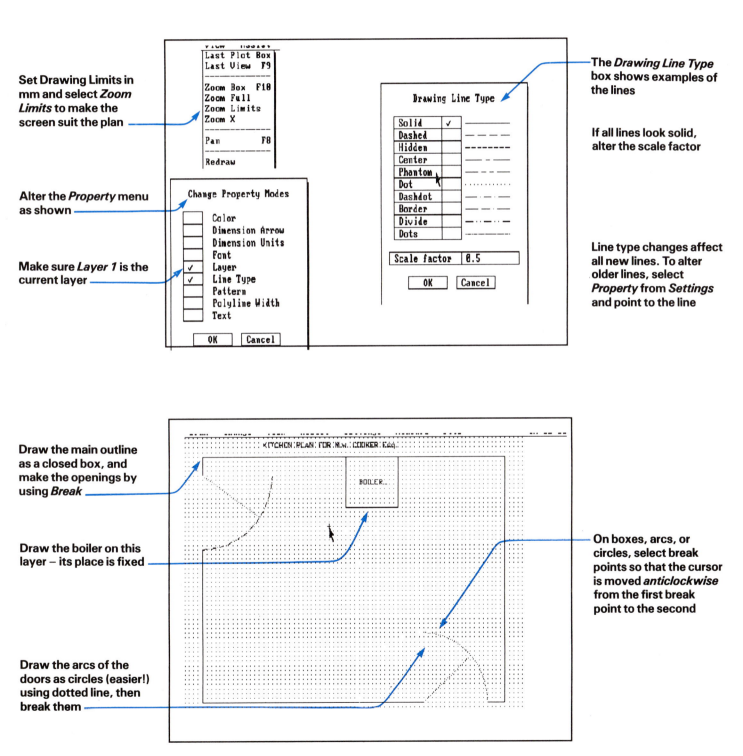

Set Drawing Limits in mm and select *Zoom Limits* to make the screen suit the plan

Alter the *Property* menu as shown

Make sure *Layer 1* is the current layer

View

Last Plot Box
Last View F9

Zoom Box F10
Zoom Full
Zoom Limits
Zoom X

Pan F8

Redraw

Change Property Modes

	Color
	Dimension Arrow
	Dimension Units
	Font
✓	Layer
✓	Line Type
	Pattern
	Polyline Width
	Text

OK Cancel

Drawing Line Type

Solid	✓	────────
Dashed		─ ─ ─ ─
Hidden		‑‑‑‑‑‑‑‑
Center		── ─ ──
Phantom		── ‑ ──
Dot		··········
Dashdot		─ · ─ ·
Border		── ─ ──
Divide		── · ──
Dots		··········

Scale factor 0.5

OK Cancel

The *Drawing Line Type* box shows examples of the lines

If all lines look solid, alter the scale factor

Line type changes affect all new lines. To alter older lines, select *Property* from *Settings* and point to the line

Draw the main outline as a closed box, and make the openings by using *Break*

Draw the boiler on this layer – its place is fixed

Draw the arcs of the doors as circles (easier!) using dotted line, then break them

KITCHEN PLAN FOR N.W. COOKER Esq.

BOILER

On boxes, arcs, or circles, select break points so that the cursor is moved *anticlockwise* from the first break point to the second

Kitchen Detail

Once the outline of the kitchen is completed and checked, add the details of furnishings on a separate layer.

On drawings of this type, one layer should be used for the main outline, one or more for detail, and another for text labels. This makes change very much easier, because work done on one layer has no effect on anything on other layers.

The Furnishings Layer

Start by selecting *Layer 2* as the current layer. The default of having all layers visible is retained, because you need to be able to see the first layer to know where to place units in the kitchen plan.

- If you are using a colour screen, you might like to draw the units in a different colour; another possibility is to use a different line type, such as dashed.
- Remember that if you change the line type you will have to alter the scale on the *Line Type* menu.
- The advantage of using a separate layer is that you can shift units about on the screen (using *Copy* or *Move*) as much as you like with no risk of interfering with the existing pattern. You might even want to place different items of fittings on different layers – with a maximum of ten layers available this presents no difficulties.
- It is often easier to draw a fitting, particularly the larger type of fitting like a sink unit, separately, group it, and move it into its final position.
- In the example, this has been done with the sink unit so that it can be tried in several places (using Copy). The unwanted versions can be erased easily if a *Group* has been made of the unit.

Shelving and Cupboards

Layer 2 has been used for the waist-level work-tops and low cupboards, and *Layer 3* for the high level cupboards; this allows for the high-level cupboards to be moved around to their best positions without any risk that lines on the lower-level will be changed.

- *Layer 4* has been used for text, the labels for the various items of kitchen furniture.

Printing the Plan

Print the plan on A4, using the default of printing the whole plan on to the specified paper. If you want to use a Plot Box, specify 15 drawing units to each plotting unit to give a suitable plot box of 279.4 mm × 201.93 mm for a drawing of a room which measures 3900 mm × 3050 mm.

Kitchen Detail

Select *Layer 2* and *Group* units like this then copy or move into place

This is on *Layer 2* with the low-level units drawn in

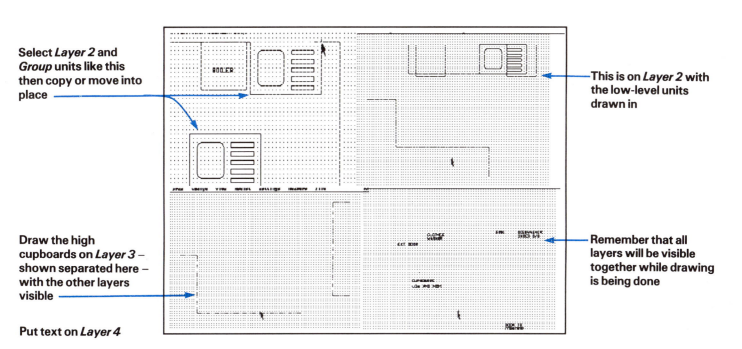

Draw the high cupboards on *Layer 3* – shown separated here – with the other layers visible

Remember that all layers will be visible together while drawing is being done

Put text on *Layer 4*

Check the complete plan with units in place on their respective layers and labels applied

Layers can be treated individually for adding fine detail or making minor corrections

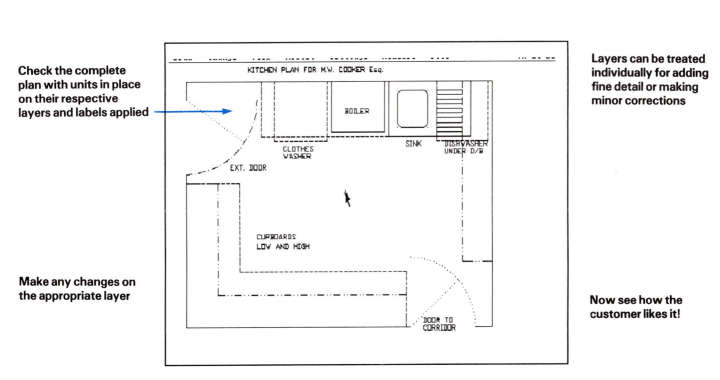

Make any changes on the appropriate layer

Now see how the customer likes it!

Zoomed Views

Zooming in AutoSketch means using the whole screen for a view of a drawing, or part of a drawing, at a different scale.

If you use Zoom to alter drawing scale in this way, you need to remember the alteration in scale if you later make an *Area Box*.

Zoom X

Use the *Zoom X* option to alter the scale of the whole drawing by a set factor. Numbers up to 1.0 will reduce the size of the drawing, numbers greater than 1.0 will increase the scale. The advantage of using *Zoom X* is that you *know* the size of the zoom factor.

Zoom Box

Select this option and use the mouse to draw a *Zoom Box*. When you click on the second corner of the box the whole screen will be used to show the area of the box, presenting a magnified view.

- You can alter Grid and/or Snaps (or turn both off) in order to make detail alterations to this part of the drawing.
- You do not know the precise scale of this Zoom, but this is not important because you will normally zoom back again.

Zoom Limits

Use *Zoom Limits* for a drawing which has used space outside the limits that were originally set. Use *Zoom Limits* to restore the screen to drawing limits, or after setting new limits. When *Zoom Full* is used, the drawing will be reduced in scale so as to fit into the screen space.

Pan

Use *Pan* (scroll bars, or from *View* menu) to see detailed views of a drawing which extends beyond the screen limits. This might be because the drawing has been made larger than the limits that were set, or because a *Zoom Box* has been used, and another part of the drawing needs to be inspected in detail without zooming back.

Zoomed Views

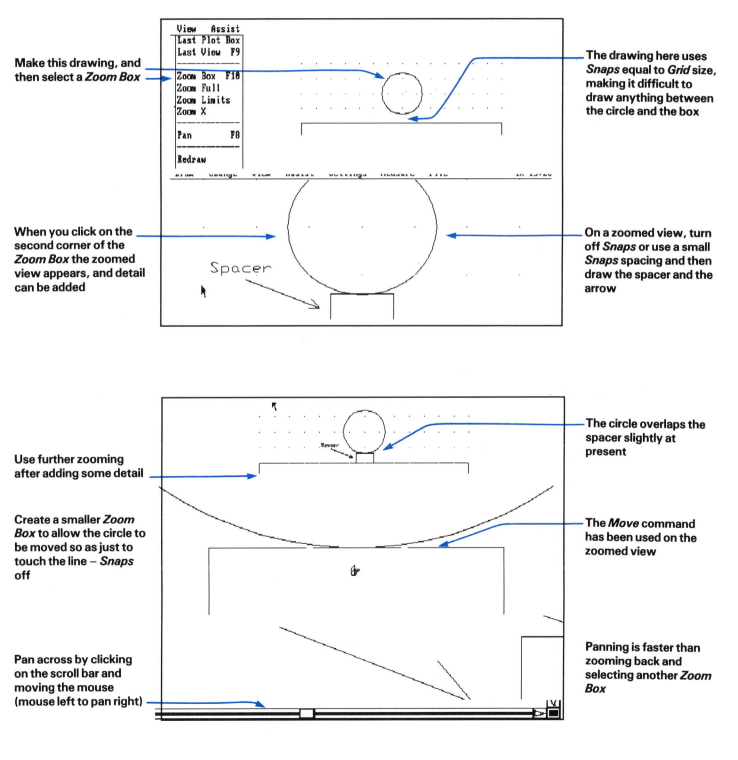

Make this drawing, and then select a *Zoom Box*

The drawing here uses *Snaps* equal to *Grid* size, making it difficult to draw anything between the circle and the box

When you click on the second corner of the *Zoom Box* the zoomed view appears, and detail can be added

On a zoomed view, turn off *Snaps* or use a small *Snaps* spacing and then draw the spacer and the arrow

Use further zooming after adding some detail

The circle overlaps the spacer slightly at present

Create a smaller *Zoom Box* to allow the circle to be moved so as just to touch the line – *Snaps* off

The *Move* command has been used on the zoomed view

Pan across by clicking on the scroll bar and moving the mouse (mouse left to pan right)

Panning is faster than zooming back and selecting another *Zoom Box*

Adding Text

The size of text characters is related to the drawing unit, and unless you are working with the defaults will always need to be changed.

- Several sets of characters or **fonts** exist. The standard font is the default, providing characters that are drawn with simple straight-line strokes.
- If you want any other fonts, you have to load them in, using the *Settings* menu. The other fonts include a mathematical set, a music set and a mapping set. Text can be selected, cut and pasted, and the Text Editor can be used like a word-processor.

Text Settings

For the *Standard* font, the only alteration needed in the Text and Font Modes menu will be to alter sizes and angles.

- The best option for *Height* is one grid spacing, in this case 5 drawing units (units are mm in the drawing). You may want to vary this when you see the text, but it makes a good starting point.
- Reduce the *Width* setting to cram more text into a given space, or increase to spread the text out.
- Use *Oblique angle* to emphasise words or phrases. *Angle* is used to make the text square up with lines which are not horizontal. In practice, it is better to have text either vertical or horizontal, not at a mixture of angles.

Using other Fonts

Select the new font from the icons, using the scroll bar if the font is not visible. Click on the **icon** and then on **OK** to load the font. You can experiment with width and oblique angle for the different fonts – reducing the width makes some fonts appear much more readable on the screen, and a small change of oblique angle can sometimes be beneficial also.

Typing the Text

Use the *Quick Text* option from the *Draw* menu to make the text appear on the screen.

- Place the cursor with the mouse, and click to establish the starting position you want to use for the text. Type a line and then press **ENTER** to end typing. If you need a new line before you end the text entry, click the mouse on the new line.
- The alternative for large amounts of text is to use the *Text Editor*. You will not then see your text appear in a font style until it is placed in the drawing.
- There are several effects that use the **%%** signs to start and stop effects:

  %%o Overscore **%%u** Underscore **%%d** degree sign **%%p** +/− symbol
  %%c Diameter dimensioning symbol **%%%** Single percent

Adding Text

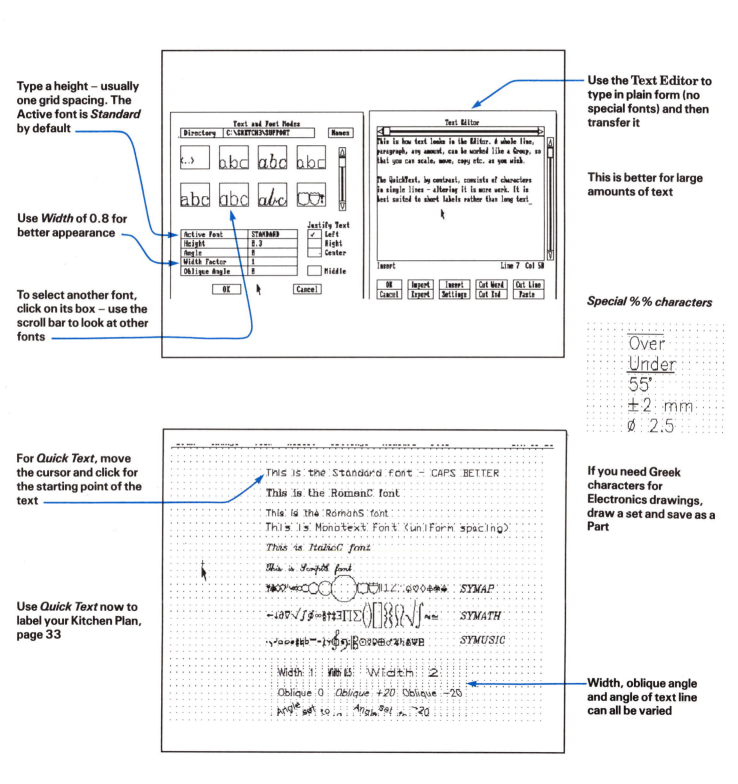

Type a height – usually one grid spacing. The Active font is *Standard* by default

Use *Width* of 0.8 for better appearance

To select another font, click on its box – use the scroll bar to look at other fonts

Use the Text Editor to type in plain form (no special fonts) and then transfer it

This is better for large amounts of text

Special % % characters

For *Quick Text*, move the cursor and click for the starting point of the text

Use *Quick Text* now to label your Kitchen Plan, page 33

If you need Greek characters for Electronics drawings, draw a set and save as a Part

Width, oblique angle and angle of text line can all be varied

Engineering Drawings

Creating an engineering drawing requires you to make use of all the techniques that you have learned to this point, and a few more that will be dealt with in the following pages. The essential points are precision of scale and correct projection.

Scale and Projection

The scale of an engineering drawing must be exact, because the drawing must show what the object will look like. The drawing need not be the same size as the object, but it should be of a simple scale factor such as 1:2 or 5:1.

- Projection refers to the two views of the object, one side-on, the other end-on. This can be made clear by the little sketch, bottom left, which indicates a side view with the small end to the left and an end-on view with the small end facing the viewer.
- A reminder of this type (which can be copied from the example) is very useful in any drawing – not all people who read engineering drawings are draughtspersons and many will have been brought up with different conventions.
- Start with straight line portions, checking for correct lengths and positions. Add curves later.
- Dimensioning is essential in an engineering drawing, but can be left until last (see page 42).

Tables

Type a table to show the title of the component, any code number, date of drawing scale, initials of persons involved and any other relevant information.

- Most firms have a house style in this respect and will expect all tables to conform – make a master and save it as a *Part* that can be imported and modified as needed.

Chamfers and Fillets

Many mechanical components have edges, that would otherwise be sharp, *chamfered* or *filleted*. The chamfer reduces the edge by cutting across at a diagonal, making two edges that are less sharp. The fillet rounds the edge into a quarter-circle.

- AutoSketch allows you to select the dimensions for chamfers or fillets (default is 0.5 units). The change is made by selecting *Chamfer* or *Fillet* from the *Changes* menu, and clicking on the two meeting lines in turn. If the lines do not meet, selecting *Chamfer* or *Fillet* will make them.

Engineering Drawings

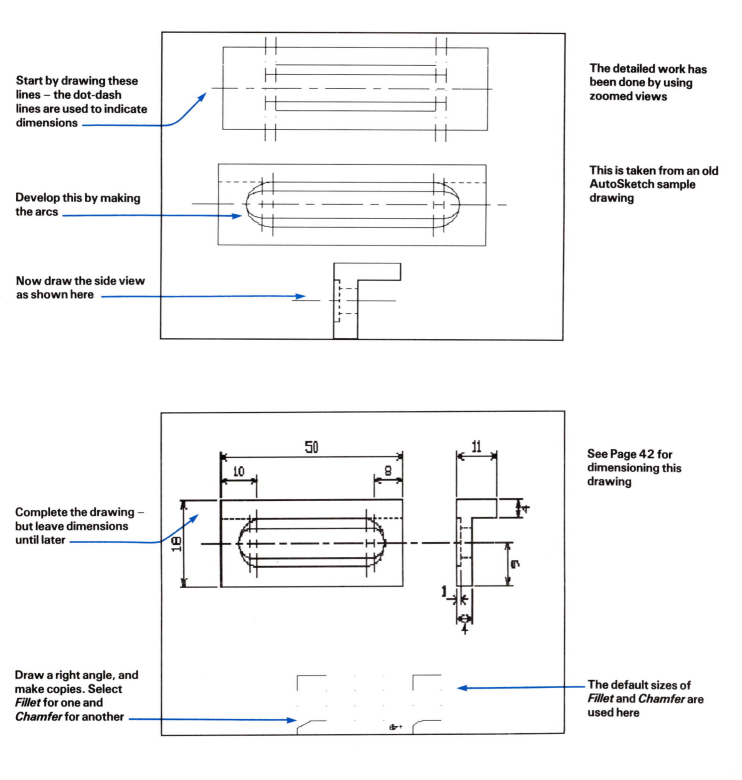

Start by drawing these lines – the dot-dash lines are used to indicate dimensions

The detailed work has been done by using zoomed views

Develop this by making the arcs

This is taken from an old AutoSketch sample drawing

Now draw the side view as shown here

Complete the drawing – but leave dimensions until later

See Page 42 for dimensioning this drawing

Draw a right angle, and make copies. Select *Fillet* for one and *Chamfer* for another

The default sizes of *Fillet* and *Chamfer* are used here

50

10

8

11

18

5

1

4

4

Drawing Details

This illustrates another of the AutoSketch examples, one that consists of considerably more detail.

- This example brings out the point that planning is as important as drawing. Starting with a simple outline on one layer, and deciding in advance how other layers will be used for detail makes the work much simpler.
- It makes the maximum use of copying, mirroring, and use of arrays to create complex shapes.

This example also uses several widths and types of lines.

- A complete drawing of this type represents a great deal of work, and this can be alleviated only if such drawings are regularly made.
- The use of arrows, for example, is much easier if a standard set of arrows are created. These can be imported as parts, and then stretched or contracted, rotated, and moved to wherever they need to be placed. This can be considerably easier if the arrows and the text are placed on a separate layer.
- All of the techniques that have been illustrated are used here, and the labelling in particular is clear and well-arranged. The use of upper-case (capital) letters avoids the problem of the poor shape of some lower-case letters. Extensive use has been made of Zooms in order to create the amount of detail which is used in this drawing.
- You should always save an elaborate drawing at intervals. AutoSketch provides for two methods of recovering from all but the worst problems when work on a drawing seems to be locked.
- If the mouse stops responding, type **Alt-M** (hold down **Alt** key, press **M** key).
- If you find that the system has locked (this may be due to a disconnected mouse or problems with the serial port) then hold down the **Alt** key and type **CRASH**. Nothing, however, replaces the requirement to make frequent backups.

Macros

AutoSketch 3.1 provides for *Macros*, which are records of all the actions involved in a drawing. These can be recorded as they are being carried out, placed in a file, and subsequently replayed. These form a particularly useful way of setting up AutoSketch in the same way each time you use it.

Drawing Details

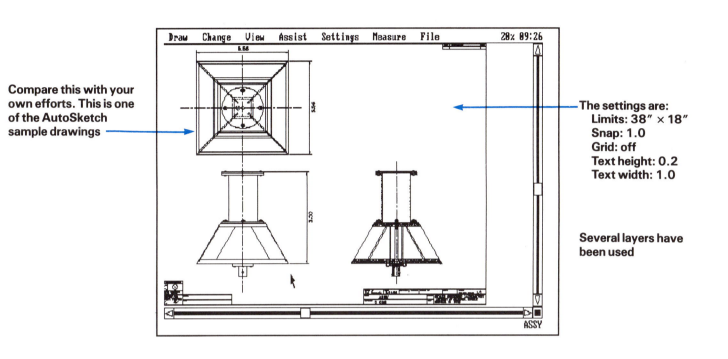

Compare this with your own efforts. This is one of the AutoSketch sample drawings

The settings are:
   Limits: 38″ × 18″
   Snap: 1.0
   Grid: off
   Text height: 0.2
   Text width: 1.0

Several layers have been used

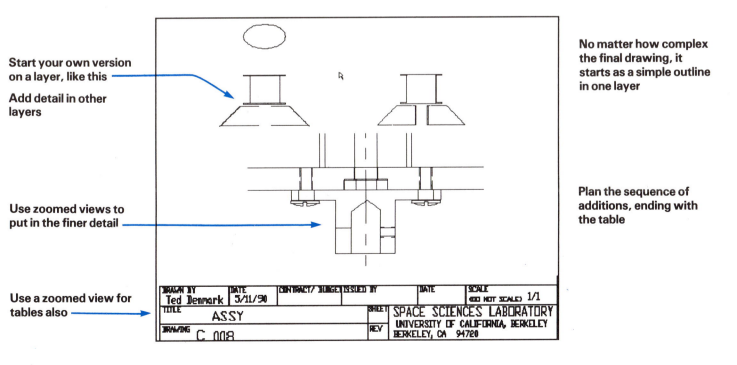

Start your own version on a layer, like this

Add detail in other layers

Use zoomed views to put in the finer detail

Use a zoomed view for tables also

No matter how complex the final drawing, it starts as a simple outline in one layer

Plan the sequence of additions, ending with the table

Measurements

Measurements

Measurements can be of two types – information temporarily put into a box, or data printed as part of the drawing. These all produce the information in a box, which disappears when you click on OK.

- For *Distance*, click on the points whose distance apart you want to find; the result is in drawing units.
- For *Angle* click on a base point (one end of a line) and then on two bearings – one of which will be the other end of the line and the other some point whose angle you want to measure. The result will be an angle in degrees, between zero and 180°.
- For *Area* click at points around the perimeter of a shape; the area is shown when you click at the first point again (which is marked).
- Select *Point* to show the co-ordinates of the pointer as you move it (like selecting *Coords*). When the button is clicked, the co-ordinates of this point are displayed in a box. This is necessary only when working in feet and inches, with non-decimal fractions.
- Select *Bearing* to measure angles to the horizontal when you click on two points of a line.

Dimensions

The *Angle, Align, Horiz* and *Vert* dimension options all produce printed data on the drawing, and you have to indicate (by clicking) where the line of print will appear (it can be moved or erased if needed).

- The *Align* dimension measures distances along a line which is at an angle, not vertical or horizontal, otherwise the meanings are all as for the measurements above. There is a choice of arrows and other dimension indicators.
- Once an object has been dimensioned, any action that changes its dimensions (such as *Stretch*) will also change the dimension data provided that this has been included inside the selection box.
- Take care to include the dimension line if a dimensioned object is moved or erased.

Filling

Select *Pattern Fill* from the *Draw* menu, and click at each point on the outline in turn.

- The fill takes place when you click back at the first point. This is easier if snaps have been used.
- For filling a curved shape, show its straight-line *Frame* to see where to click the mouse. The filling is part of the object and will be erased with the object.

Measurements

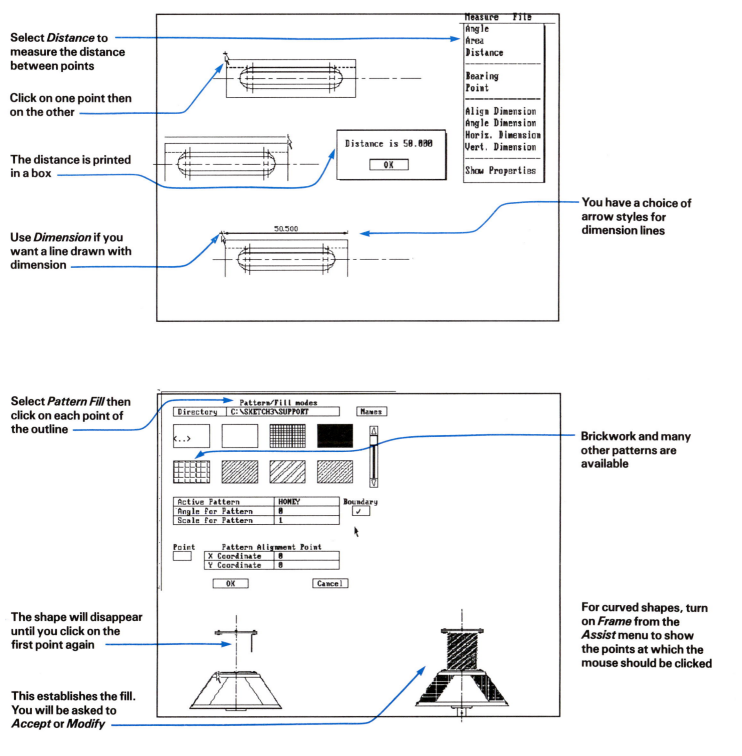

Select *Distance* to measure the distance between points

Click on one point then on the other

The distance is printed in a box

Use *Dimension* if you want a line drawn with dimension

Measure File
Angle
Area
Distance
─────────
Bearing
Point
─────────
Align Dimension
Angle Dimension
Horiz. Dimension
Vert. Dimension
─────────
Show Properties

Distance is 50.000
[OK]

50.500

You have a choice of arrow styles for dimension lines

Select *Pattern Fill* then click on each point of the outline

Pattern/Fill modes
Directory C:\SKETCH3\SUPPORT   Names

Active Pattern   HONEY   Boundary
Angle for Pattern   0   [✓]
Scale for Pattern   1

Point   Pattern Alignment Point
[ ]   X Coordinate   0
       Y Coordinate   0
       [OK]   [Cancel]

Brickwork and many other patterns are available

The shape will disappear until you click on the first point again

This establishes the fill. You will be asked to *Accept* or *Modify*

For curved shapes, turn on *Frame* from the *Assist* menu to show the points at which the mouse should be clicked

AUTOCAD Compatibility

AutoCAD is the big-brother program of AutoSketch, a fully-featured CAD program whose price reflects its capabilities. AutoCAD is the program for professional users who will be using large plotters (A3 upwards) and whose investment in hardware and software will be from £10,000 upwards.

- One of the considerable advantages of AutoSketch is that its files are compatible with those of AutoCAD, assuming that the version of AutoCAD is reasonably up to date.
- The transfer is done by a type of file referred to as DXF (Drawing Exchange Format); this type of file also allows AutoCAD information to be used in AutoSketch. DXF files can also be used to transfer drawings to some DTP programs.

Transferring AutoSketch files to AutoCAD

The AutoSketch file should exist in its standard form as a disk file whose extension letters will be SKD, for example, **MTNBIKE2. SKD**, **ENGINE. SKD**.

- Use *Open* from the *File* menu to read the SKD file from your disk, so that the drawing shows on the screen.
- Select *Make DXF*. Use the same main filename, or change the name if you want to. You can use a filename that includes another drive or directory.
- Click on **OK** to create the file. The message DXF Out appears while the file is being created.
- Use the DXF file in AutoCAD, following the instructions in the AutoCAD manual.

Transferring AutoCAD files to AutoSketch

Create a DXF file from your AutoCAD file, following the instructions in the AUTOCAD manual.

- Start AutoSketch, and select *Read DXF* from the *File* menu
- Fill in names for Directory (such as B:\ or C:\DRAW) and click on **OK**
- Select the file name when it appears (use Page Up or Down on a long list)
- Click on **OK** when the file is selected.
- The drawing will appear after some time – the message *DXF In* is at the foot of the screen during the waiting period.
- If the drawing is not visible when the *DXF In* message disappears, use *Zoom Full* from the *View* menu to see the drawing. You will probably need to make a new Plot box to plot this drawing.
- Because AutoCAD is a more capable program than AutoSketch, some drawings may not transfer entirely in their original form. The type of drawings that can be made using AutoSketch, if they have been created in AutoCAD, will transfer without problems, but drawings which include AutoCAD features that are absent in AutoSketch, such as 3-D views, will transfer ignoring these features.

Using Drawings in DTP

Drawings that you have made using AutoSketch can be copied in the normal way for reproduction in publications, using normal paste-up methods. If you want to include such drawings into work that is produced by Desk-Top Publishing you need to convert the AutoSketch files into a form that can be used by the DTP system. This is not necessarily easy, because some DTP systems make little or no provision for importing AutoSketch files

● There are two main methods of passing AutoSketch drawings to DTP programs, the use of SLD files and the use of ADI plotter files. The method that you use depends on the type of files that your DTP package can read.

Slide Files

AutoSketch contains in its *File* menu the option *Make Slide*. Select this while a drawing is on the screen, and specify a drive/directory in the usual way for the file, which will have the extension letters of SLD.

● This is different type of file, one which resembles the files created by Paint-type programs – it specifies position and colours of dots rather than the start and end of lines.
● Your DTP package may be able to read SLD files directly – consult the manual for the DTP package on this.
● Your DTP package may include a converter program which will convert SLD files into one of the more common formats such as TIF or PCX.
● You can buy converter programs, such as OPTIKS (from the Public Domain Software Library) which can convert SLD files into other formats.

Plotter Files

Another way of passing AutoSketch drawings to DTP is to make use of a plotter file. This method works well with Aldus PageMaker, one of the most popular of the 'heavyweight' DTP programs.

● Reconfigure AutoSketch, selecting *ADI Plotter* (either) and *Binary File*.
● When the drawing is on screen, make a suitable Plot box.
● Plot, providing a suitable filename (drive/directory as required).
● This will produce a file with the PLT extension which can be read by PageMaker.

These two methods should be applicable to many of the better-known DTP packages, but for many users, finding a suitable converter may be a problem. Only the most recent version of OPTIKS lists the SLD type of file as one of its standard formats. A commercial program, Metafile, from ZenoGraphics, will convert from DXF files into the CGM format, if your DTP package can use CGM files.

45

Final Points

In this book some items have been omitted mainly because they were not immediately essential to the understanding of AutoSketch. These are dealt with very briefly here.

Start-up Configuration.

It is not always convenient to have to alter drawing limits, grids, snaps, etc. each time a drawing is started. If your normal defaults are very different from those of AutoSketch, the simplest solution is to create a blank drawing called DEFAULT or A4 (for example) which has been created with the limits, grids, snaps and other settings you want to use.

- Load this drawing when you start work, and use *Save As* when your work is complete, so that you use another name. Make the DEFAULT file a read-only one (see any good book on DOS for details) to protect it, or read it from a write-protected floppy disk.

- You can also use a Macro to carry out a set of actions when AutoSketch is started. Remember also that the function keys, alone, or with **Alt** or **Ctrl**, can be used for fast selection of actions.

SKETCH.CFG File

The configuration of your AutoSketch program is determined by a file called SKETCH.CFG. If you sometimes want to use AutoSketch to plot directly and sometimes to plot to disk (for subsequent DTP use), it can be handy to keep two such files.

- Rename the existing SKETCH.CFG as CFG1 and create another one (by using SKETCH /R) and rename it as CFG2. Depending on which one you want to use, rename as SKETCH.CFG before you start SKETCH running. The renaming can be done in a batch file, for example:

```
CD\SKETCH
REN CFG1 SKETCH.CFG
SKETCH
REN SKETCH.CFG CFG1
CD\
```

– calling this file SKPLOT, and using another similar batch file with CFG2 in place of CFG1 called CFGDTP (to start Sketch for direct plotting or for DTP respectively).

Size and Memory

AutoSketch 3.1 can create drawings that are twice as large as was possible using AutoSketch V.2. This requires your computer to be fitted with expanded (not extended) memory (or using software that allows extended memory to be used like expanded memory) of up to 2 Mb.